Front cover illustration by Rick Penn-Kraus

A Guy Goes to the Doctor...

The World's Best Doctor Jokes

According to Bob Fraser

PRICE STERN SLOAN
Los Angeles

Front cover illustration by Rick Penn-Kraus

Copyright 1992 by Bob Fraser

Published by Price Stern Sloan, Inc.
11150 Olympic Boulevard, Suite 650
Los Angeles, CA 90064

Printed in MEXICO
10 9 8 7 6 5 4 3 2 1

All rights reserved. No part of this publication may be reproduced, stored in a retrieval system or transmitted in any form or by any means, electronic, mechanical, photocopying, recording or otherwise, without the prior written permission of the publisher.

Library of Congress Catalog Card Number: 91-066241
ISBN: 0-8431-2858-5

NOTICE: The information contained in this book is true and complete to the best of our knowledge. All recommendations are made without any guarantees on the part of the author or of Price Stern Sloan, Inc. The author and publisher disclaim all liability in connection with the use of this information.

Foreword

I love doctors.

I point this out in case I get sick some day.

Now for the foreword.

No one knows the history of doctor jokes, but I think it's safe to say they've been around since Hippocrates was a pup.

The alert reader will note that there are several jokes included about psychiatrists. This is because shrinks are doctors too. (Many New Yorkers seem to think that they are a necessity—like water, electricity and *The Daily News*.)

This book is dedicated to my family, without whom many doctors and dentists would have to curtail their fancy vacations. It is also dedicated to those caring, loving individuals who have chosen to pursue a medical career—I refer, of course, to malpractice attorneys.

But mostly it is dedicated to joke-tellers—those wonderful people who make long car trips, the army and boring parlor games tolerable.

The foreword is over. Turn the page.

A GUY GOES TO THE DOCTOR suffering from the most horrible headaches.

The doctor has bad news. "In order to get rid of these headaches you'll have to be castrated."

The guy is naturally upset at the prospect, but he can't stand the headaches any longer and agrees to the procedure. The doctor operates and the guy feels just great.

He feels so good he decides to go on vacation.

He goes to a very expensive tailor to buy a vacation wardrobe. The tailor takes one look at him and says,

"Don't tell me, I know your sizes. Jacket: a size 42. Pants: a size 36. Shirt: a size 16-34. And underwear: a size 36."

The guy is impressed. "You're exactly right, except for the underwear. I wear size 34 underwear."

"This is not possible," says the tailor.

"But I've been wearing size 34 for years!" says the guy.

"Really?" says the tailor. "I'm surprised you don't get the most horrible headaches."

A GUY GOES TO THE DOCTOR with an odd complaint.

"I've been seeing spots in front of my eyes."

"Ah. Mmm. Have you seen another doctor?"

"No, just spots."

A GUY GOES TO THE DOCTOR and tells him that he wants a vasectomy.

The doctor agrees to perform the procedure but asks if the guy is sure that this is what he wants.

"Have you discussed the operation with your family?"

"Oh, sure," says the guy. "In fact, we took a vote on it."

"What was the outcome?" asked the doctor.

"The kids favored it, eleven to three."

A GAL GOES TO THE DOCTOR with a delicate problem.

After the exam, the gynecologist shakes his head.

"I'm sorry, miss, but removal of that vibrator is going to involve a very expensive operation!"

"I don't know if I can afford that," says the woman. "Can you just replace the batteries?"

A GUY GOES TO THE SAME PSYCHIATRIST for ten years.

One day the shrink has good news.

"Oh, Doctor, do you mean I'm cured of my kleptomania? I don't know how I can ever repay you."

"You've paid my fee. That's all I expect. However, if you happen to suffer a relapse, I could use a new Walkman."

A GUY GOES TO THE DOCTOR.

"Doctor, I don't know what's wrong with me. Every morning at six, just like clockwork, I have a bowel movement."

"What's wrong with that?"

"I don't get out of bed until eight thirty."

A GUY GOES TO THE DOCTOR for his annual checkup.

His wife sits in the waiting room.

After about forty-five minutes, the doctor comes out to chat with the wife.

"I don't like the looks of your husband."

"Neither do I, but he's good to the children."

A GUY GOES TO THE DOCTOR with a big problem.

Or rather a little problem that won't get any bigger.

The doctor tells him the bad news.

"You're impotent."

The guy is naturally upset.

But the doctor gives him a new miracle drug and tells him to put two drops in his food and not to miss a meal.

The next night the guy's at a restaurant with his girl and he's forgotten to use his drops at lunch.

He waves the waiter over and explains the situation.

"You'd better put four drops in my soup. In fact, just to be on the safe side, make it six drops."

The waiter nods and leaves for the kitchen.

Twenty minutes go by and the guy is beginning to wonder where his soup is.

Finally he excuses himself and goes to find his waiter.

"Where is my soup?" asks the guy.

The waiter shrugs. "The cook thinks we should wait for the noodles to lie down."

A GUY GOES TO THE DOCTOR complaining about his sex life.

"My wife and I have been married ten years and lately she doesn't seem interested."

The doctor understands and gives him some pills.

"Tonight before you go to sleep," the doctor says, "drop one in her coffee."

The guy follows the doctor's orders and puts a pill in her coffee—and then, just to be on the safe side, he puts a pill into his own coffee. Later, while they're watching TV, the wife jumps on her husband, moaning. "I want a man! I want a man!"

The guy pushes her away, also moaning.

"So do I! So do I!"

A GUY GOES TO THE DOCTOR.

"I keep dreaming that Kirstie Alley is trying to seduce me and I push her away."

"What would you have me do?"

"Could you break my arms?"

A GUY GOES TO THE DOCTOR.

> His wife is going to have a baby.
>
> "This is our first kid, Doc. And one thing I'm worried about—how long after she has the baby can we make love again?"
>
> "Well," says the doctor, "that really depends on whether she's in a ward or a private room."

A GUY GOES TO THE DOCTOR.

> He is bloody and battered.
>
> "What happened?" asks the doctor
>
> "I got seenus trouble."
>
> "You mean sinus, don't you?"
>
> "No," moans the guy. "I was boffing my wife's best friend, and she seen us!"

A GUY GOES TO THE DOCTOR with a delicate problem.

> The gorgeous receptionist asks the guy what his problem is—so she can fill in his forms.
>
> "It's rather embarrassing," the guy mutters, "but I have an extremely large sexual organ and it's in an almost constant state of arousal."
>
> "Well, the doctor is very busy today," she coos, "but maybe *I* can squeeze you in."

A GUY GOES TO THE DOCTOR with his wife.

"She's not feeling tip-top, Doc," says the guy.

The doctor examines the woman and says, "Well, this is serious. You two are going to have to stop having sex. Any more sex and this woman may die."

The guy says he'll sleep downstairs and the wife agrees that that might be best.

So he sleeps downstairs for three nights.

On the fourth night he can't sleep, so he gets up and heads upstairs.

And meets her coming *down*.

She says, "I'm just coming downstairs to die."

He says, "That's funny, I was just coming upstairs to kill you."

A WOMAN GOES TO A DOCTOR.

During the examination, he notices that one of her breasts is three inches longer than the other.

"How did this happen?"

"My husband sleeps with it in his mouth."

"That wouldn't do it, ma'am."

"We sleep in twin beds."

A GUY GOES TO THE DOCTOR for an examination.

After the exam the guy is putting his clothes back on.

The doctor says, "I've got some good news and some bad news."

"Give me the bad news, Doc. I can take it," says the guy.

"Well," says the doctor, "you've got untreatable nerve disease, your heart is murmuring and your hair is falling out in the back."

"What's the good news?"

"I broke eighty at the country club yesterday."

A GUY GOES TO THE DOCTOR with a stomach problem.

"What did you eat for dinner last night?" the doctor wants to know.

"Oysters," says the guy.

"Fresh oysters?"

"How can you tell if they're fresh?"

"Couldn't you tell when you took off the shells?"

"Oh no! You're supposed to take off the shells?"

A GUY GOES TO THE DOCTOR with a sore throat.

"Doc, you're charging me forty dollars? All you did was paint my throat!"

"What did you expect for forty dollars? Wallpaper?"

A GUY GOES TO THE DOCTOR.

"Ever since we moved to L.A., our sex life has fallen apart. What's the problem?"

After examining the man, the doctor advises him, "Jog ten miles a day, every day for seven days—then phone me."

A week later, the guy phones.

"Well," says the doctor, "has the jogging improved your sex life?"

"Not really. I'm in Bakersfield."

A GUY GOES TO THE DOCTOR with his wife, grumbling.

"Look," says the wife, "if you don't want to get a vasectomy, just say so. I'll go back on the pill."

"It's not that," says the guy. "I just wish you hadn't told the kids you were going to get me *fixed*."

A GUY GOES TO HIS OPTOMETRIST.

The doctor has new offices. Featured in the waiting room is a ten-foot-by-ten-foot oil painting of a human eye.

The guy is looking at the painting when the doctor comes out.

"You think it's too much?" asks the doctor.

"Oh no," says the guy. "I'm just glad you're not my proctologist."

A GUY GOES TO THE DOCTOR complaining about his sex life.

He can't seem to get it hard and keep it that way.

The doctor nods and gives him a prescription for drops.

But the pharmacist goofs and writes the dosage on the label as thirty drops instead of three.

The guy's wife shows up in the doctor's waiting room a week later.

"How nice to see you," says the doctor. "Did those drops I gave your husband do the trick?"

"Oh, they worked all right," she says. "What we need now is an antidote, so they can close the coffin."

A guy goes to the doctor. He's very old but in great condition.

The doctor praises his good health and the old guy begins to brag.

"About four weeks ago," he said, "I met an 18-year-old girl who took me to the beach and made love to me all night.

"Three weeks ago, I picked up a 20-year-old at Sears and we went to her car and did it for three hours.

"Just last week, I grabbed a 26-year-old, took her to the Hilton and we've been making love for six straight days."

"My God, man! All these strange girls—I hope you're using some kind of precaution!"

"Of course," says the old guy. "I give them a phony name and address."

A lady goes to her doctor with a question.

"Are birth control pills tax-deductible?" she asks.

"Only if they don't work."

A GUY GOES TO THE DOCTOR complaining of stuttering. It's driving his wife nuts.

The doctor examines him and has bad news.

"It's your penis. It's the longest one I've ever seen. It's so heavy that it's pulling on your vocal cords and that's what's causing you to stutter."

"B-b-but, w-w-what c-c-can you d-do t-to help m-m-me?"

"I'll have to cut part of it off."

After the operation, the guy talks perfectly, but his wife misses her husband's Promethean equipment and insists he get it put back on.

The guy goes back to the doctor and says, "I don't care if I do stutter. I'd rather have my manhood back."

And the doctor says, "T-t-t-too l-l-late n-n-n-now!"

A GUY GOES TO THE DOCTOR without an appointment.

The nurse says she can schedule him in two weeks.

"Two weeks? In two weeks I could be dead!"

"In that case," says the nurse, "please have the courtesy to call and cancel the appointment."

A GUY GOES TO THE DOCTOR.

"I'm seventy and my girlfriend is sixty-six and we think we may have lost the spark. Could you watch us make love and see if you can spot any problems?"

"Certainly," says the doctor. "Bring your girlfriend into the office. I have a quiet room you can use where I'll be able to observe."

So the old couple returns. They use the room and the doctor observes.

"You're making love perfectly," says the doctor. "That will be $18."

Two weeks later, they're back and he watches them again, and again assures them that they are doing everything right, and again charges them eighteen dollars.

Two more weeks go by and they return.

"Why do you keep coming back?" asks the doctor. "I told you you're making love properly."

"Well," the guy says, "she can't come to my house and I can't go to her house, and a motel costs $40. You only charge us $18 and we get $15 back from Medicare."

A LADY GOES TO THE DOCTOR with an odd problem.

"Doctor, everytime I sneeze, I have an orgasm," says the lady.

"What are you taking for it?"

"Black pepper."

A GUY GOES TO THE DOCTOR and says that he is afraid his teenage son has come down with V.D.

"He says he hasn't had sex with anyone but the maid, so it had to be her."

"Don't worry," says the doctor. "Send him in to the office."

"I will, Doctor," says the guy. "But the problem is, I've been to bed with the maid myself and I have the same symptoms."

"That *is* too bad."

"Not only that, I think I've passed it on to my wife."

"Oh no!" says the doctor. "That means we all have it."

A GUY GOES TO THE DOCTOR complaining of chronic constipation.

The doctor gives him some suppositories.

"If they don't help," says the doctor, "come back in a week."

In a week the guy is back—his constipation is worse.

"Did you use the suppositories?" asks the doctor.

"Of course I did," answers the patient. "I took one every night with my orange juice."

"You swallowed the suppositories?"

"What the hell do you think I did—stick 'em up my ass?"

A GUY GOES TO A PSYCHIATRIST.

The shrink asks the guy, "What do you do for a living?"

"I'm a mechanic. I work on cars."

"Fine," says the shrink. "Get under the couch."

A GUY GOES TO THE DOCTOR, worried about his inability to have an erection.

"How old are you?" asks the doctor.

"Ninety," says the guy.

The doctor chuckles. "When did you first notice your incapacity?"

"Just this morning. I got to thinking about it."

"Look," says the doctor, "you're much too old for this sort of thing. There's nothing I can do to resurrect the past."

"Then please, Doc, can you do something to stop me from thinking about it?"

A LADY GOES TO A PSYCHIATRIST to complain about her husband.

"He thinks he's a refrigerator. You can see what it's doing to me. I haven't had a decent night's sleep in months."

"My good woman, you won't do your husband any good by staying up all night worrying about his condition."

"I'm not worried about his condition. He sleeps with his mouth open and that damn little light is keeping me awake."

A GUY GOES TO THE DOCTOR with a pain in his chest.

It turns out the guy is lucky and came to the doctor just in time.

The doctor checks him into the hospital and performs a triple bypass operation on the guy's heart.

The guy wakes up from the operation and is happy to find out it was successful.

He asks the doctor, "Will I be able to indulge in sexual activity?"

"Yes," says the doctor, "but you should limit it to your wife. We don't want you getting too excited."

A LADY GOES TO THE DOCTOR for her annual physical.

That evening in an attempt to arouse her husband, she tells him about her exam.

"The doctor said I had flawless skin. And he said my breasts were magnificent and that my legs were classic."

"Did he mention your big fat ass?" asks the husband.

"No," says the lady, "your name never came up."

A GUY GOES TO A PSYCHIATRIST.

"Doc, I've got a problem. All I ever dream about is baseball. Baseball, baseball, baseball."

"Don't you ever dream about girls?"

"I wouldn't dare," says the guy. "I might lose my turn at bat."

A GUY GOES TO THE DOCTOR.

"I just can't find a cause for your illness," says the doctor. "I think it's due to drinking."

"In that case, I'll come back when you're sober."

A LADY GOES TO HER VET complaining about her very large dog.

"The minute I walk into the house he jumps up and starts humping away at me. Is there anything you can do?"

"Well," muses the vet, "I suppose I could castrate him. Then he wouldn't have much of a sex drive."

"Gee, that seems harsh. Couldn't you just clip his nails and do something about his breath?"

A GUY GOES TO THE DENTIST.

He hates dentists and hasn't been to one in thirty years.

The dentist looks at him and says, "Your mouth is a wreck. I've got at least five weeks worth of work here."

"Doc, I gotta tell you—I can't stand pain."

The dentist is wounded. "Who said anything about pain? I did a job exactly like this for another man. You call him. Ask if there was any pain." So the guy phones.

"Listen," he says, "I'm here at the dentist and he says he did a big job on your mouth. Was there any pain?"

"Maybe this story will give you some idea," says the guy on the other end. "He finished with me two years ago. Now, just this last Sunday I took my wife to the park and we went out on the lake in a boat. We're just floating along when suddenly one of the oars falls overboard. I reach out to grab the oar and get my scrotum caught in the oarlock ... and would you believe it, that was the first time in two years that my damn teeth didn't hurt!"

A GUY GOES TO THE DOCTOR feeling listless.

The doctor tells the guy, "You're ninety years old. You should be in a nursing home."

Arrangements are made and the guy is moved into a home with 24-hour-a-day nursing care.

The guy sits outside to get some sun.

After a few moments he starts to lean to the left.

The nurse catches him by the shoulder and pushes him upright.

A few moments later he starts to lean to the right.

Again the nurse pushes him upright.

This goes on all afternoon.

He leans. She pushes.

That evening the doctor visits the guy and asks how he's being treated.

"Well, the food is good. The room is nice. But the nurse won't let me fart."

A LADY GOES TO A PSYCHIATRIST.

"I think I'm a nymphomaniac."

"I see," says the shrink. "I think you should know that my fee is fifty dollars an hour."

"How much for all night?"

A GUY GOES TO THE DOCTOR worried about his sex life.

The doctor encourages the man to undergo self-hypnosis training.

Sure enough, after a few sessions with the doctor, the guy's wife notices a big improvment in the bedroom.

She knows that hypnotism is involved, but is curious about how it works. So the next night she sneaks into the bathroom to watch her husband do his thing in front of the mirror.

The guy is swinging a pocket watch back and forth and chanting to himself, "She's not my wife. She's not my wife."

A GUY GOES TO THE DOCTOR.

The doctor asks, "How old are you?"

The guy says, "Seventy-seven."

"And how often do you have sex?"

"I'd say once a week."

"You're seventy-seven, and have sex once a week? What are you complaining about?"

"Well," says the guy, "my neighbor is eighty-one and he says he has sex twice a week."

"So? You say the same thing!"

A GUY GOES TO THE DOCTOR and demands to be castrated.

"What? Why in the world ...?"

"Don't ask questions, Doc," says the guy. "Just castrate me. Here's the money."

Shrugging his shoulders, the doctor performs the deed.

As the guy is coming around, the doctor says, "Listen, as long as the anesthetic is still working, why not get yourself circumcised?"

"Dammit! That's the word! I wanted to be circumcised!"

A GUY GOES TO A PSYCHIATRIST.

"Look, Doc," says the guy, "I don't want to go through analysis, but I'll pay you $500 to answer two questions."

"That's rather unusual," says the shrink, "but I"ll go along with it."

"Is it possible," says the guy, "for a normal man to be in love with an elephant?"

"Impossible. I've never heard of it in all the annals of psychiatry. What's the second question?"

"Do you know anyone who wants to sell a wedding gown—size 88?"

A GUY GOES TO THE DOCTOR.

The doctor examines him and tells him that his pulse rate is very high.

"Well, I've been thinking about sex a lot lately," the guy giggles.

"I see. And how often do you have sex?"

"Once a year."

"You have sex only once a year? No wonder your blood pressure is so high."

The guy grins at the doctor.

"Mister, this could be life or death. I think you should try to wipe the smile off your face."

"I'd love to, Doc, but tonight's the night!"

A GUY GOES TO A PSYCHIATRIST.

"Doctor, I think I'm a dog."

"So you think you are a dog, eh? Well, lie down on the couch and we'll talk about it."

"I couldn't do that, Doctor. I'm not allowed on the furniture."

A GUY GOES TO THE DOCTOR, worried.

"Doc," he said, "I feel like killing my wife. You've got to help me."

"Murder is a bad idea," says the doctor. "I have a better idea. I'll give you these pills. They will allow you to make love to your wife six times a day. In thirty days you'll love her to death."

"Great idea, Doc. I'll take her to Hawaii so she won't be suspicious."

A few weeks later the doctor happens to go to Hawaii and who does he see coming along the beach in a wheelchair, but his patient.

The guy is a wreck, a shell of a man, a wasted husk of humanity. Strolling along beside him is a gorgeous redhead.

"What happened?" whispers the doctor to the guy.

"Don't worry about me, Doc," says the guy. "She's the one you should feel sorry for."

"Your wife?"

"Yeah. Little does she know that tomorrow she dies!"

A BEAUTIFUL LADY GOES TO A PSYCHIATRIST.

"It's liquor, doctor. Whenever I have a drink I just have to make love."

"I see," says the shrink. "That's a neurotic compulsive behavior. Please lie down on the couch. Can I get you a cocktail?"

A GUY GOES TO THE FAMILY DOCTOR.

"My father has recently won the lottery," says the guy. "But as you know, he has a bad heart and I'm afraid if I tell him the good news, the surprise would kill him."

"Let me handle it," says the doctor.

So the doctor chats with the father for a while and then sort of casually asks, "By the way, I hear you bought a lottery ticket. Is that so?"

"Yes, I did," says the father.

"Forty million is certainly a lot of money. Have you thought of what you'd do with the money?"

"Doc, you've always taken care of this family—and if I win the lottery, half goes to you."

The doctor drops dead.

A GUY GOES TO A PSYCHIATRIST.

"I'm in love with my horse," says the guy. "I desire my horse!"

"I see," says the shrink. "What kind of horse is it? Male or female?"

"Female, of course! Do I look like some sort of pervert?"

A GUY GOES TO A PSYCHIATRIST.

"Doc, you've got to help me. I can't remember anything. Not what happened a year ago, or even what happened yesterday. I'm worried, Doc."

"Hmmm. How long have you had this problem?" asks the shrink.

"What problem?"

A GUY GOES TO THE DOCTOR for his physical.

He takes off all his clothes.

The doctor is stunned. "Jeez, man, you've got three male organs!"

The guy's a little sheepish. "I know."

"How do your pants fit?"

"Like a glove!"

A GUY GOES TO THE DOCTOR.

"My wife and I just can't seem to complete the sex act. We've tried and tried."

"You're putting too much pressure on yourself," says the doctor. "You need to relax and just let it happen. Just forget about it until you feel the urge. Then, no matter what you're doing, sweep it aside and make love."

"Okay, Doc."

Two weeks later the doctor sees the guy at the mall.

"Did my advice work for you?" asks the doctor.

"Oh, yes, Doctor. Wonderfully. Last week, at dinner, my wife and I reached for the salad at the same time and our hands touched. There was this electricity. So we swept the salad aside, stripped off our clothes and we made love right there on the table. It was glorious."

"That's wonderful," says the doctor.

"Of course, we can never go back to Denny's again."

A GUY GOES TO THE DOCTOR for his physical.

The doctor says, "You're in perfect health."

The guy steps into the next room.

The doctor hears a crash and rushes in to see the guy lying on the floor—flat on his face.

The nurse says, "He just fell right over."

The doctor checks the guy.

"This guy's dead. Quick, Nurse, grab his feet."

"Why, Doctor?"

"We've got to turn him around—make it look like he was coming *in*."

A GUY GOES TO A PSYCHIATRIST.

He is dressed like Napoleon.

"Doc, I need your help," says the guy.

"I can see that. Tell me your problem."

"I don't have a problem! I'm the emperor of France. I am rich and powerful and ready to conquer the known world. But I'm afraid my wife, Josephine, is in real emotional trouble."

"What makes you think so?"

"Well, for one thing, she keeps insisting that she's a Mrs. Pinsky."

A GUY GOES TO A PSYCHIATRIST.

He wants to know if marrying an octopus would be considered the act of a sane man.

The shrink is thunderstruck. "Marry an octopus? I would consider that the act of a raving lunatic."

"Damn! What am I going to do with eight engagement rings?"

A GUY GOES TO A PSYCHIATRIST.

"I am Arnold Schwarzenegger," says the guy.

The doctor tries a little experiment and puts the guy in a padded cell with another man who thinks *he's* Arnold Schwarzenegger.

The next morning he looks in on the two men.

"Who are you?" he asks the first guy.

"Doctor, I realize now that I have been suffering from a delusion. I'm *not* Arnold Schwarzenegger."

"Good. And do you know who you are?"

"Yes," says the guy demurely, "I'm Maria Shriver."

A GUY GOES TO THE DOCTOR with his wife.

"She's a nymphomaniac, Doc. Maybe you can do something for her? She goes for any man, and I get very jealous."

"I'll do what I can," says the doctor.

He takes the luscious Mrs. into his examining room, closes the door, tells her to undress and get up on the table.

The moment he touches her, she begins to moan and squirm.

It's just too much for the doctor, who climbs up and begins to make love to her.

The guy, hearing moans and groans coming from the examination room, goes to see what's up. He sees the doctor astride his wife.

The doctor is quick. "Oh, it's you. I'm taking your wife's temperature!"

The guy draws a pistol from his pocket.

"Okay, Doc," he says, "but when you take that thing out, it better have numbers on it!"

A GUY GOES TO A PSYCHIATRIST.

"I want a second opinion," says the guy. "My fancy-schmancy doctor over on Park Avenue says that I am in love with my Water-Pik. Have you ever heard of such a thing?"

"That's pretty unusual," agreed the doctor.

"I mean, sure we have a certain amount of affection for each other—but love? Ridiculous!"

A GUY GOES TO THE PSYCHIATRIST.

"What can I do for you?" says the doctor.

"People," says the guy. "The whole damn human race is so stupid and stubborn."

"I see," says the doctor. "And what is it that people do that upsets you so much?"

"They call me crazy, Doctor. I suggest that there are ways of doing things—they say *I'm* crazy! They won't listen to a word of truth."

"Why don't you start at the beginning," says the doctor.

"Okay," says the guy. "In the beginning, I created the heavens and the earth. And the earth was without form and void ..."

A GUY GOES TO THE PSYCHIATRIST.

"Doctor," says the guy, "I feel as if I'm two different people. Two totally different personalities. Do you think I need help? Can you help me? Am I doing the right thing seeing a psychiatrist?"

"Whoah," says the doc. "One at a time."

A WOMAN GOES TO THE DOCTOR with a weight problem.

The doctor tells her that she can lose a lot of weight by wrapping her nude body in Saran Wrap.

The woman thinks it's odd, but agrees to try it.

That night her husband comes home to find her lying on the couch—wrapped in Saran Wrap.

He takes one look at her and says, "Oh no, leftovers again."

A GUY GOES TO THE DOCTOR complaining about feeling listless and weary.

After a few questions the doctor suggests that the guy give up half his sex life.

"Which half, Doc?" asks the guy. "Talking about it—or thinking about it?"

A WOMAN GOES TO THE DOCTOR.

After examining the woman thoroughly, the doctor is perplexed.

"I'm not sure what it is," the doctor says. "You either have a bad cold or you're pregnant."

"Oh," says the woman, "I must be pregnant—I don't know anyone who could have given me a cold."

A GUY GOES TO THE DOCTOR to get a physical for a trip around the world.

The doctor says, "I'm not sure a trip around the world is such a good idea. You're not a well man."

"But I need this trip, Doc. I need the adventure, the excitement and the beautiful women! Doc, I'm going on this trip—and don't try to stop me."

"Who's going to stop you?" says the doctor. "I'll go with you."

A WOMAN GOES TO THE DOCTOR complaining that she gets a terrible pain in the groin every time it rains or snows.

"How tall are you?" asks the Doc.

"Almost four feet," says the woman.

"I see," muses the doctor. "I'd like you to come back to the office the next time it rains or snows."

She does. He has her lie down on the examining table for a few minutes and then asks her to get up and walk around.

"How do you feel now?" asks the Doc.

"Oh, much better," says the woman. "What did you do, Doctor?"

"I just cut four inches off the top of your galoshes."

A GUY GOES TO THE DOCTOR complaining of hearing loss.

The doctor examines him and says he wants to fix the guy up with a new hearing aid.

"This is the finest hearing aid now being manufactured. I wear one myself," says the doctor.

"What kind is it?" asks the guy.

"About half past four."

A GUY GOES TO THE DOCTOR complaining of burnout.

The doctor suggests that the guy get some time away from work.

The guy comes back a month later and still feels terrible.

"Did you take my advice?" asks the doctor.

"Well," says the guy, "a friend of mine invited me up to his cabin in the woods. A quiet, secluded place with no nightlife, no parties and not a woman within a hundred miles."

"And that didn't help?"

"Who went?"

A GUY GOES TO THE DOCTOR complaining of feeling listless.

"How old are you?" asks the doctor.

"Sixty-six," says the guy.

"And your wife, how old is she?"

"Well I just re-married, Doc. My new bride is twenty-two."

"I see," muses the doc.

"So, what do you think? Am I overweight?"

"No, just over-matched."

A GUY GOES TO THE DOCTOR.

> The doctor examines the guy and asks, "Could you pay for an operation if I thought one was necessary?"
>
> The guy thinks a minute.
>
> "Would you think an operation was necessary if I couldn't pay for it?"

A WOMAN GOES TO A PSYCHIATRIST.

> "It's my son, Doc. He's always making mud pies."
>
> "I see," says the shrink. "I think you're worrying yourself needlessly. Mud pies are a perfectly normal outlet for tactile exploration."
>
> "Well, I *am* worried—and so is his wife."

A GUY GOES TO THE DOCTOR.

> "I feel funny, Doc. What should I do?"
>
> "Go on television."

A GUY GOES TO THE DOCTOR with a gunshot wound.

> "Are you shot bad?"
>
> "You ever know anybody who was shot good?"

A GUY GOES TO THE DOCTOR.

"I feel terrible, Doc. I'm always depressed."

"Mmm," says the doc. "Aren't you the weatherman on channel five?"

"Yes, I am the weatherman."

"In that case, I suggest you move to another area of the country."

"Move? Why?"

"Because the climate around here doesn't agree with you."

A GUY GOES TO A PSYCHIATRIST.

"Doc, you gotta help me. I'm acting like a dog. I bark at cars, eat my dinner out of a bowl on the floor and pee on the front lawn."

"Mmm," says the shrink. "And how long has this been going on?"

"Ever since I was a puppy."

A GUY GOES TO THE DOCTOR.

The doctor examines the man and asks, "Do you live a normal life?"

"Of course," answers the guy.

"Well, you'll have to cut it out."

A WOMAN GOES TO A PSYCHIATRIST.

"It's my son, Doctor. He plays Nintendo® all day long. I can't even get him away from it to eat or sleep. I'm worried."

"Well," says the shrink, "I don't usually make house calls—but in your case ..."

Sure enough, there's the kid playing Nintendo® with a glassy look on his face.

The shrink goes over and whispers in the boy's ear.

The boy immediately switches off the Nintendo® and leaves the room.

"How did you do it?" asks the woman.

"Simple," says the shrink. "I just told your son to turn off the Nintendo® or I'd beat the crap out of him."

A GUY GOES TO THE VETERINARIAN.

"I want you to cut my dog's tail off," says the guy.

"Why do you want your dog's tail cut off?"

"Well, my mother-in-law is coming to visit and I don't want anything in the house to suggest that she's welcome."

A GUY GOES TO A PSYCHIATRIST.

"Doc, I've got a problem."

"Yes? And exactly what is your problem?"

"Well, I'm married with three kids. I have a new car. My wife has a new car. Two of my kids have new cars. We have a house in the city and vacation home in the mountains. We have a boat, a large screen TV and all the latest gadgets."

"I still don't see your problem," says the shrink.

"I only make seventy bucks a week."

A GUY GOES TO THE DOCTOR.

After a thorough examination, the doctor tells the guy that he is going to have to undergo surgery.

"But let me tell you right away how I work," says the doctor. "I believe in getting my patients up and around immediately following surgery. One hour after the operation you'll be up and about and after two hours you'll be home, and after lunch you should return to work. Any questions?"

"Will you let me lie down during the operation?"

A WOMAN GOES TO THE DOCTOR with a little weight problem.

The doctor examines her and gives her a slip of paper.

"If you follow my instructions, I guarantee that you will lose weight," says the doc. "And you can eat anything you want."

"Really? I can eat anything I want?"

"Yes. But you can't swallow."

A GUY GOES TO A PSYCHIATRIST.

"My wife made me come. I don't know why," says the guy.

With that, the guy begins to stuff pipe tobacco in his left ear.

The shrink watches this procedure for a moment and then agrees that the guy has come to the right place.

"There must be some way I can help you," says the shrink.

"Sure, Doc," says the guy, tilting his head. "You can give me a light."

A GUY GOES TO THE DOCTOR.

After an examination the doctor gives the guy the bad news.

"But Doc," pleads the guy, "I can't afford expensive surgery right now. And I definitely can't afford to take time off of work to recover from it. Isn't there something else you can do?"

"Well," muses the doc, "I guess I could touch up the X rays."

A WOMAN GOES TO THE DOCTOR with a weight problem.

The doctor examines her and gives her a very large bottle of very small pills.

"How often do I take the pills?" asks the woman.

"Oh, you don't take them," says the doc. "Three times a day you spill them on the floor and pick them up one by one."

A GUY GOES TO A PSYCHIATRIST.

The shrink asks the guy, "Do you have trouble making up your mind?"

"Well," says the guy, "yes and no."

A GUY GOES TO THE DOCTOR.

"It's just a cold," says the doc. "Not much I can do for you."

"But Doc, I'm miserable. There must be some way to help me."

"Well, all right. Go home, take a hot bath and while you're still wet, go outside and roll around on the ground for a few minutes. Then run around the block three times in your bathing suit."

"Geez, Doc, it's thirty degrees out. I'll catch pneumonia."

"Indeed. But I can cure pneumonia."

A GUY GOES TO THE DOCTOR with assorted bruises, contusions and broken bones.

"What happened to you?" asks the doctor.

"It was a silly mistake, Doc," says the guy. "I was a little tipsy last night and when I got home I began to make love to my wife. I wasn't thinking and said, 'You're really something, honey. You make love just like my wife.'"

A GUY GOES TO THE DOCTOR, who immediately checks him into the hospital.

The hospital is a disaster.

Lousy food, nasty nurses and no TV.

The guy is miserable.

The doctor comes in the next week and tells the guy that he has some bad news.

"Go ahead, Doc, I can take it," gulps the guy.

"I'm afraid you only have 24 hours to live."

"Thank God," says the guy. "I thought you were going to tell me I had to stay in this place another week."

A GUY GOES TO THE DOCTOR.

"I don't know if you can help me, Doctor, but I can't seem to remember people's names."

"Actually," says the doctor, "the best way to remember a name is to use a memory hook. For instance, if you meet a man named Baker, you might think of bread—and remember baker. Or if his name is Silver, you might think of earrings."

"I see," says the guy. "But suppose I meet a guy named Farnskippytuthalter?"

"Go back and talk to Baker."

A GUY GOES TO THE DOCTOR.

"I'm so unhappy, Doc. I can't find a woman to complete my life."

"Well," muses the doctor, "my suggestion is to advertise in one of those singles columns. Look for a woman who likes to do the same things you like to do."

"What am I going to do with a woman who likes to whistle at girls?"

A GUY GOES TO THE DOCTOR.

He is suffering from multiple contusions, bruises and fractured small bones.

"My gosh!" exclaims the doctor. "What happened to you?"

"My wife beat me up."

"Why?"

"I spoke."

"Your wife did this to you just because you spoke?"

"Well, no—I forgot to raise my hand."

A WOMAN GOES TO THE DOCTOR.

She has gone through five boyfriends in as many months.

"What am I going to do, Doctor?" pleads the lady. "It's my complexion, I know it is. I've been wrinkled before my time."

"Perhaps corrective surgery ..."

"No, Doctor, I can't afford that."

"Well, I do have this new untested cream that is guaranteed to take the wrinkles out of prunes—maybe you'd like to try that?"

"I'll try anything," says the woman.

And she goes off with a jar of the special cream.

She's back two weeks later.

"It isn't working, Doctor. I still can't hold onto a man—although I do have the smoothest prunes in town."

A GUY GOES TO THE DOCTOR.

"Doctor, I can't pee."

"How old are you?" asks the doc.

"I'm eighty-nine," says the guy.

"You've peed enough."

A GUY GOES TO A PSYCHIATRIST.

"I don't understand the problem," says the Doctor. "You're a famous movie star with hit records, a charming girlfriend and from what I understand, quite a lot of money."

"Ahh money!" snarls the guy. "What good is money to me? Here I am with everything and my poor mother is starving in a cardboard house down by the docks!"

A GUY GOES TO A DOCTOR.

"My Lord!" shouts the doctor. "What happened to you?"

"I was out duck hunting with my buddies and I accidently shot myself in the groin."

The doctor struggles for hours to get all the buckshot out of the man's privates.

Finally finished, the doctor tells the guy, "I think you'd better find the best piccolo player in town."

"Why?" asks the guy.

"Well, somebody has to teach you to finger that thing so you don't pee all over yourself."

A LADY CALLS THE DOCTOR.

"My little boy found a bullet and swallowed it," she cries.

"Well," muses the doctor, "I guess the best thing to do is give him a very strong laxative—and for two or three hours make sure you don't point him at anyone."

A GUY GOES TO THE DOCTOR.

He's huffing and puffing as he comes into the office.

"Doc, I just can't seem to get my breath. What's wrong with me?"

"You're fat, you smoke like a locomotive, you're stupid and you're in the wrong office. I'm a lawyer."

A GUY GOES TO THE DOCTOR.

"Well," says the doctor, "you're anemic and you need nutritional supplements."

"I'd like a second opinion, Doc."

"Okay—I think you're ugly too."

A LADY GOES TO THE DOCTOR.

>She's ninety if she's a day.
>
>She begins to flirt with the doctor as he asks his questions.
>
>Finished with the preliminaries, the doctor tells the woman to disrobe.
>
>"Take off my clothes?" she moans. "All right, Doctor, but I'm warning you, you're playing with fire."

A LADY GOES TO THE DOCTOR.

>After an exam, the doctor says, "You can tell your husband that you're going to have a baby."
>
>"I don't have a husband."
>
>"Oh, well, then tell your lover."
>
>"I never had a lover, Doctor."
>
>"Oh, well, then go home and wait for a star to appear in the east."

A GUY GOES TO A PSYCHIATRIST.

He tells the doctor that he thinks he's a dog.

"A dog, eh? Well, we shall see about that."

The guy goes to treatments with the shrink for years.

Then one day he's walking along and meets an old friend.

One day the doc asks, "How are you feeling today?"

"Oh, I'm in great shape. Tip-top. Go ahead, feel my nose."

A GUY GOES TO THE DOCTOR.

He's ninety-something and has married a 20-year-old woman.

"Should I take any special precautions?" asks the guy.

"Take in a boarder," says the doc, winking.

A couple of months later, the guy's back.

"My wife is pregnant."

"Oh," says the doctor, "perhaps taking in a boarder wasn't such a good idea."

"You're telling me. The boarder is pregnant too!"

A GUY GOES TO THE DOCTOR.

>The doctor looks a little concerned.
>
>"I'm afraid you're going to have to have a small procedure."
>
>"An operation?" moans the guy. "How much will it cost?"
>
>"Six hundred dollars."
>
>"Is it dangerous?"
>
>"No, you can't get a dangerous operation for six hundred dollars."

A LADY GOES TO THE DENTIST.

>"My dentures don't fit," she complains.
>
>The dentist checks everything, working in her mouth for about an hour.
>
>"Ma'am, these teeth seem to fit perfectly."
>
>"Sure, in my mouth. What about the glass?"

A GUY GOES TO THE DOCTOR.

"I'm having trouble sleeping, Doc. And my boss is getting pretty upset with my listlessness at work."

"Take one of these tonight, and tomorrow you should wake up refreshed," says the doctor.

Well, the guy figures if one pill is good, then two pills would be terrific.

Sure enough, when morning arrives, the guy hops out of bed feeling fabulous. He showers, shaves, has a big breakfast and gets to work at ten to nine.

"I feel great!" the guy tells the boss. "I'm full of pep and ready to rumble!"

"That's fine," says the boss, "but where were you yesterday?"

A GUY GOES TO THE DOCTOR.

"I'm afraid I have some bad news," says the doc. "You might go at any minute."

"Thank God," says the guy. "I haven't gone in five days."

A GUY GOES TO A PSYCHIATRIST.

He labors under the delusion that he is Abraham Lincoln.

"I think my wife is trying to get rid of me."

"What makes you think that?" asks the doctor.

"She keeps trying to get me to go to the theater."